TANGLED LIGHT

A Collection of Poems and Songs

Brian Mackenzie

WORDCATCHERpublishing

Tangled Light
A Collection of Poems and Songs
Wordcatcher Modern Poetry

© 2019 Brian Mackenzie
© Mike Hurry for front cover image
Cover design © 2019 David Norrington

British Library Cataloguing in Publication Data.
A catalogue record for this book is available from the British Library.

Published in the United Kingdom by Wordcatcher Publishing Group Ltd
www.wordcatcher.com
Tel: 02921 888321
Facebook.com/WordcatcherPublishing

First Edition: 2019

Print edition ISBN: 9781789422801
Ebook edition ISBN: 9781789423235

Category: Poetry

For Kristelle and Ripley

Thanks to Mike Hurry for his fabulous picture
that I have used for the front cover.
It was taken in Reelig Glen, Moniack
near Inverness in Scotland.

Contents

INTRODUCTION 1

WINTER CHILL 2

NO COLOURS 4

I WHISPER TO THE WIND 6

ROSE TINTED GLASSES.................................9

THE BLACK TRENCH COAT 10

THESE REDWOOD TREES 12

DEVIL'S KISS 13

THIS CREEP.. 14

PEACE FI DE CHILDREN................................ 16

PEACE FOR THE CHILDREN.......................... 17

TANGLED LIGHT 18

DARK CLOUDS... 20

MYSTIC BLUE.. 22

SILENTLY RUNNING 23

SEAWEED RUM 24

WIND ON MY FACE....................................... 26

A SITHEAN 28

DESERT LIFE 30

BODY BAG.. 32

ONE SUNDAY MORNING............................... 34

MY DARLING FRIEND................................... 36

SILVER DARLINGS.. 38

PEIRA CAVA... 40

BALLAD OF THE MOON................................ 42

TOURS OF DUTY 44

A SON'S FATHER 46

A BIT OF DIRT 48

CRITICAL MASS 49

SHIVER AND CHILL 50

THE SWEETEST MISTRESS............................... 52

BLACK HOLES 54

THE VILLAGE GREEN 55

CRUEL ENVY 56

INVISIBLE CAGE 57

IN A WAR THAT THEY WON............................... 58

HEY BILLY... 60

CHILDREN YOU GOT TO STOP 62

SLEEPING ROUGH 64

WAR ZONES 65

THE TEARS I HIDE 66

LOTUS FLOWER 68

WHO WE ARE 70

PANTA SANTA... 72

A DARK SHADE OF BLUE................................. 74

KING RAT LA LOTTE 75

ANCIENT LOVE 76

HOUDINI'S PUNCH... 78

YOUR MOTHER'S ARMS................................... 80

NO CHRISTMAS TIME IN DIXIE 82

LORD PROTECT OUR LOVE 85

THE PRISON.. 86

I'LL BE HERE FOR YOU 87

S.O.S. 88

ALL THE KING'S HORSES... 90

THE TOWER... 92

NEVER MEANT TO BE 94

PLATO O PLOMO 96

LOVE NEVER COMPETES 98

DANCE WITH ME... 100

BPC 102

IT DOESN'T MATTER IF IT RAINS................................. 104

FIRE IN HIS EYES 106

ABOUT THE AUTHOR 107

INTRODUCTION

Happiness, pain, breakup, lies, lust and laughter. The ups and downs of relationships including the darkness and depression that is rarely spoken of. But it isn't all doom and gloom, with the lows come the highs and humour to keep us going! Tangled Light holds poems and songs about the vast spectrum of love that we can all relate to.

I am pleased to say that some of my songs have been adapted, recorded and released by the fabulous Desert Life and are available at all the normal channels.

WINTER CHILL

there is nothing to feel
but the cold winter chill
the bleak wind it rages
and drifts up the snow
a cold starving cougar
left foot prints behind
she's hunting for food
when it's fifteen below

if all this bad
open and raw
would just go away
in the spring time thaw

there is nothing to win
in Gods forsaken place
just numbs your senses
with cheap whiskey rot
it's another young girl
found frozen in snow
a sweet soul is taken
that's escaped her lot

there is no day goes by
you hide from your loss
just accept it's your fate
in the cold winter chill
it's time for moving on
numb all your thoughts
the cold starving cougar
at last makes her kill

if all this bad
open and raw
would just go away
in the spring time thaw

Adapted for song

there is nothing to feel
but the cold winter chill
the bleak wind it rages
as it drifts up the hill

a cold starving cougar
left foot prints behind
she's hunting for food
there is nothing to find

there is nothing to win
in Gods forsaken place
just numbs your senses
with cheap whiskey lace

it's another young girl
found frozen in snow
a sweet soul is taken
that had nowhere to go

there is no day goes by
you hide that your lost
just accept it's your fate
in the cold winter frost

it's time for moving on
the last of your will
cold starving cougar
she at last makes a kill

if all this bad
open and raw
would just disappear
in the spring time thaw

NO COLOURS

No flames of shimmering orange glow
pink, purple and poppies red
no forty shades of forest greens
all eyes are grey in their heads

lego bricks look the same
strawberries taste of grey
my favourite skittle hard to find
all the balloons pale away

when you left and went away
you drained my colours
left me here in black and white
and many shades of grey

No sunsets of brilliantly sparkling hue
indigo, lilac and baby blue
all my flowers they blossom drab
paradise birds colourless flew

Christmas lights are a bore
lavender smells of grey
you can't see kites in the sky
rainbows have gone away

when you left and went away
you drained my colours
left me here in black and white
and many shades of grey

No crimson flames fuel fires bright
saffron, peach and candy pink
no Joseph's coat of many colours
coral reefs are dead I think

cherry blossom are so drab
ruby lips look like grey
a spicy pizza does not invite
the carnival is not so gay

when you left and went away
you drained my colours
left me here in black and white
and many shades of grey

I WHISPER TO THE WIND

I'm lost in the ocean
the wind is the law
body bleached and ravished
my hands are raw
lost my sales
lashed by waves
surrounded by whales
look up I see stars
there's swells, sharks
currents and calm
dragging me down
every turn is so far

I don't think I'll make it
I'm losing my will
losing my fear

whisper the words I want to hear
whisper to the wind my love

I'm lost in the jungle
it's humid and hot
blood drained by mosquitoes
my feet they rot
bitten by fleas
strangled in vines
surrounded by trees
my bed is the fern
there's jaguars, scorpions
spiders and snakes
blocking my path
every way that I turn

I don't think I'll make it
I'm losing my will
losing my fear

whisper the words I want to hear
whisper to the wind my love

Updated for song

lost in the ocean
the wind is the law
I'm surrounded by sea
my hands are raw
I have lost my sails
I'm followed by whales

I whisper that I love you
I whisper to the wind

lost in the jungle
Its humid and hot
I'm surrounded by trees
my feet they rot
for my mistakes
I'm chased by snakes

I whisper that I love you
I whisper to the wind

high in the mountain
I'm bitten by frost
I'm surrounded by snow
I'm lonely and lost
the snow it shifts
I'm covered in drifts

I whisper that I love you
I whisper to the wind

lost in the dessert
blinding white heat
I'm surrounded by sand
it burns my feet
quick as you blink
I would kill to drink

I whisper that I love you
I whisper to the wind

lost in our home
without you it's bare
I'm surrounded by memories
we used to share
for all of your lies
I've said goodbyes

I whisper that I love you
I whisper to the wind

lost in an earthquake
the earth it breaks
I'm surrounded by panic
my head it shakes
for all my fails
It's off the scales

I whisper that I love you
I whisper to the wind

ROSE TINTED GLASSES

we rose from the dust
and these ashes of loss
marched to the sounds
of military bands
the Fuhrer's voice
rang in our ears
he gave us the future
filled us with hope

I saw my man
through rose tinted glasses
in his black uniform
he looked like a god

with our mythical past
aligned with the Gods
the red Swastika flags
sway in the wind
the Fuhrer's voice
rang in our ears
he gave us his vision
1000 year Reich

I saw my man
through rose tinted glasses
in his black uniform
he looked like a god

the silver skull
shone like a fire
death and destruction
burning our land

THE BLACK TRENCH COAT

She wanted to spread her wings
(*her thighs*)
it was January, it was winter cold
I was alone in my dungeon
the single bar heater gave little warmth
Songs of Love and Hate arrived today
it was on repeat
a bottle was on the table
two fingers of comfort were left
the words *'Jane came by with a lock of your hair'*
stung, they stung in my grieving ears
the cigarette smoke froze in the cold
the bottle stood empty
the room slowed down

I needed a drink
I slipped on my 'famous' Black Trench coat
I headed for the door, the night, the biting rain
searching for a bar, searching for anywhere
wanting her

She wanted to have her freedom
(*sleep with men*)
the bar was warm, it was bright
I stood alone at the bar
I asked for a beer and a whiskey to chase
the juke box was busy and playing loud
it was country tunes
my empty glasses
needed a quick refresh
the words '*I won't come in while he's there*'
stung, they stung in my grieving ears
the light mixed with the smoke
people had no faces
voices were a drone

I needed a drink
I slipped on my 'famous' Black Trench coat
I headed for the door, the night, the biting rain
searching for a bar, searching for anywhere
wanting her

She wanted to move on
(*be with him*)
I entered to the sounds of life
bright lights and pounding noise
I ordered a cocktail
a Manhattan with a beer assist
White Russian, a High Ball helper
it was disco music
my empty glasses
they cried out for more
the words '*I give you all a boy could give*'
ripped, they ripped through my grieving ears
flashing lights screamed
puppets were dancing
where was oblivion?

I needed a drink
I slipped on my 'famous' Black Trench coat
I headed for the door, the night, the biting rain
searching for a bar, searching for anywhere
wanting her

THESE REDWOOD TREES

50 degrees in Al Nahda Park
drag me to the Wheat
all the buildings reach for the sky
trying to escape the heat
always there for every day
the redwood trees stand tall and proud
guarding the Longlands Way

you made the choice
it was yours to call
you choose the riches
of these green fields
turning your back
on the glitter ball

in the distance Burj Khalifa
head on to the Goose
the Irish Village a comfort brings
with secrets in their juice
always there on your side
the redwood trees stand tall and proud
guarding the Heatherside

heart of the Palm Atlantis
in the Carpenters Arms
the greatest mall that ever lived
with its gifts and charms
it took one thousand years
these redwood trees stand tall and proud
guarding all your fears

you made the choice
it was yours to call
you choose the riches
of these green fields
turning your back
on the glitter ball

DEVIL'S KISS

I'm lost in the darkness
can't find any way home
I'm hounded and followed
and feel so alone

every rustle and noise
all the walls closing in
any shadow that moves
I panic within

in this deep pit
the dark abyss
my lips brushed
by the devil's kiss

I am scared of the night
can't find peace in the day
in sleep there are demons
I can't keep at bay

head spins and turns
all remorse and regret
the mists get darker
I can't forget

in this deep pit
the dark abyss
my lips brushed
by the devil's kiss

THIS CREEP

this fog creeps under my door
into my room
and soon
I'm surrounded by gloom
it goes into my mouth
my nose, my ears
into my brain
clouds my thoughts
clouds my eyes
clouds my fears

got no life
I'm under the knife
can't walk, can't drink
can't eat, cant think
got no life

this dark creeps under my door
into my bed
my head
I'm surrounded by dread
it takes over my cheer
my guts, my voice
into my brain
darkens my thoughts
darkens my eyes
darkens my fear

this disease creeps under my door
into my lung
my tongue
the place where I am hung
it takes over my rear
my colon, my liver
into my throat
infects my thoughts
infects my eyes
infects my fear

got no life
I'm under the knife
can't walk, can't drink
can't eat, cant think
got no life

PEACE FI DE CHILDREN

wi dont want yuh war
just gi wi food to ave
fi wi kids a starvin
dem tire an cryin

dem live wid di sound
of di dying young men
all di horra round
it normal fi dem

peace fi de children
let dem run an play
peace fi di children
allow dem grow tall

tap di stabbin and fightin
killin everyone
all the drugs an Yardis
leave fi wi children alone

can wi be happy
black beans pond Sunday
wid aal fi wi fambily
laugtha an song

peace fi de children
let dem run an play
peace fi di children
allow dem grow tall

PEACE FOR THE CHILDREN

we don't want your war
just give us food to eat
our kids are starving
they're tired and beat

they live with the sound
of the dying young men
all the horror around
it's normal for them

peace for the children
let them run and play
peace for the children
allow them to grow tall

stop the stabbing and fighting
killing everyman
all the drugs and Yardis
leave our children alone

can we be happy
black beans on Sunday
with all our family
laughter and song

peace for the children
let them run and play
peace for the children

TANGLED LIGHT

what is love?
they say it's blind I'm told
something you can't see
something you can't even hold

who is God?
he lives in heaven I believe
someone we made up
someone who can help us grieve

what is a soul?
it is supposed to live on
could it be just a spark
a flick of a switch and it's gone

are we lost on a satellite
spinning around in an endless night
are we lost on a satellite
our love is lost
from the candle light

what has past
can it ever be changed?
or is it there forever
tied to its resting place

who am I
a guy who lost to you
now I'm lost in space
someone without a clue

are we lost on a satellite
spinning around in an endless night
are we lost on a satellite
our love is lost
from the candle light

are we lost on a satellite
in a meaningless spin
love I believe
is only tangled light

DARK CLOUDS

enter the room
dark clouds around
an atmosphere
electric charged

your brow down
your eyes glazed
the words I say
will be attacked

with dark clouds around you

I am the reason
for all this pain
because of me
your life in ruins

guilt bites hard
to feel this bad
is it me you see
in front of you?

with dark clouds around you

web closing in
a chainless trap
to walk away
unthinkable act

keeping strong
not dragged in
have to remain
be here for you

with dark clouds around me

if it's me
then I will go
but if you wish
I will stay

if I cause
all this sorrow
I must leave
I'll walk away

with dark clouds around me

MYSTIC BLUE

when it's night
I have to stare
my love has moonbeams
in her hair
I see stardust everywhere
magic is in the air

I swear
don't know what to do
when she smiles
it's mystic blue

when it's day
I say a prayer
my love has rainbows
in her hair
I see sunshine everywhere
love is in the air

I swear
don't know what to do
when she smiles
it's mystic blue

at night
she's surrounded
by sparkling fireflies
in the day
the coloured kites wave
as she passes by
all the flowers bloom
rain drops on her skin
smell of sweet perfume

I swear
don't know what to do
when she smiles
it's mystic blue

SILENTLY RUNNING

Hungry grey wolves
hunting in packs
with ruthless cunning
stalk their prey
sleekest of lines
silently running
beneath the waves

Sieg heil!, sieg heil!
to our hero's at sea
Iron crosses await
for the deeds they have done
another merchant ship
blown up to the sea
four hundred souls
screaming and drowning
to their dark hellish death

crammed in a hull
forty brave men
depth charge explode
lights go out
dark closing in
silently running
waiting for death

SEAWEED RUM

Animal crackling

Ah! gimme a tot of seaweed rum
need more me hearties, to see the gig
from the menu eel eye pie
they say the drummer's a porky pig
bo diddley trotter
it's ok to fly!

Ah! gimme a tot of seaweed rum
need more me hearties, to see the gig
from the menu hedgehog quill
they say on bass is a slimy squid
half step inky
it's ok to shrill!

Ah! gimme more that seaweed rum
need more me hearties, to see the gig
from the menu slug in cream
they say the lead is a grizzly bear
ol' baloo fret
it's ok to scream!

Ah! gimme more that seaweed rum
need more me hearties, to see the gig
from the menu snake rat cake
they say the singer is a beluga whale
blubbering blobby
it's ok to shake!

Ah! can't get enough of seaweed rum
need more me hearties, to see the gig
from the menu toad wart soup
on tambourine it's a horny gazelle
bambi jingle
it's ok to whoop!

Ah can't get enough of seaweed rum
need more me hearties, to see the gig
from the menu stinky otter cheese
on glockenspiel it's a stingy bee
honey chili buzz
it's ok to tease

Ah can't get enough of seaweed rum
need more me hearties, to see the gig
from the menu beaver stew
the say on trumpet is a baby roo
blow Joey jumper
are you ok blue

WIND ON MY FACE

A Middle eastern threat
little babies born
to mothers on run
in need of shelter
desperate for food
please give them help
and stop this feud

what have I got to be unhappy about
when I can walk to the front
watch the tide coming in
see the waves as they race
touch the rain falling down
feel the wind on my face

Ebola virus disease
an all Africa time bomb
countries on knees
villages wiped out
desperate suffering
too much to endure
search for a vaccine
give them a cure

Cancer it's creeping
it's an all world crisis
people weakening
sentence of death
chemicals or drugs
oncologist's mission
all hoping for time
or any remission

Mosquito Virus Zica
the all American's hell
a mothers' stigma
babies are born
heads all shrunk
brains misshapen
with not any cure
a future is taken

Human traffic horror
is big business today
many girls to sell
there to be used
is it the trafficker
who is to blame
or is it the punter
his lustful shame

what have I got to be unhappy about
when I can walk to the front
watch the tide coming in
see the waves as the race
touch the rain falling down
feel the wind on my face

A SITHEAN

Hill of fairies

wake in the morning
the sight of wonder
she's there before us
the hill of the fairies

souls aimlessly walk
in ghostly shadows
kept in their chains
under locks and key

she gives us shelter
protects us all
from the north sea winds

born in the ice age
down through time
far did she travelled
to find peaceful rest

with an eerie silence
no bird would settle
In her constant pain
they all torment her

when eight bridges cross
there will be fire and water
rage through the city
down through the streets

the battle was over
there for our prince
provide with shelter
his safe haven to go

two fiddlers played
their futures passed
when bell ring tolled
they turned to dust

there waiting below
Fingal's army sleeps
he's awaiting the call
for a country's peril

she gives us shelter
protects us all
from the north sea winds

DESERT LIFE

Scorched is the earth
my loves barren land
wind whistle lightly
through the Rio Grande

these days hang
with screaming white heat
nights endless desolation
cold bitterness deep

my love taken by Indians
marauders they flee
shimmering horizons
she's a mirage that I see

follow the trail
along a sidewinders path
the bleached white skulls
are the oasis wrath

the atmosphere heavy
you could slice with a knife
vultures pick the bones
of the desert life

she is lost to the desert
a bride to the sands
I will search forever
through unforgiving land

death rattles tail
a coyote bitch screams
black scorpion stings
lost withered dreams

oh! sweet darling Sheree
I see the eagles fly
whispers in the wind
and your vision in the sky

lizards scuttling
the desert owl's flight
a loud eerie silence
for the devil tonight

the atmosphere heavy
you could slice with a knife
vultures pick the bones
of the desert life

BODY BAG

Salute to the flag

well done leader man
you got your war
time for the payback
to those who put you there
get all the soldier boys
comrades in arms
fight for their country
proud of their flag

take the hand from your heart
your names on a body bag

one bullet one dollar
you do the maths
whose got the contract

proud for your son
like dad before
born to the army
we know what it takes
if you don't come home
we fill with pride
you took their bullet
standing there tall

take the hand from your heart
your names on the honour wall

one bullet one dollar
you do the maths
whose got the contract?

we kill the bad guys
Gods on our side
we kill the bad guys
Gods on our side

stand tall
for the leader man
salute to the flag
take the hand from your heart
your names on a body bag
your names on the honour wall

ONE SUNDAY MORNING

I wake in the morning
no clouds outside
the sun is shining
with no place to hide

enjoying the silence
with no need to talk
my dog is hassling
she's wants her walk

stroll down the sand
I throw her a stick
the sea is coming
she's got to be quick

smelling the breeze
she takes in the air
retrieves her stick
with nothing to care

It's one Sunday morning
you feel you're alive
this world can be good
a place to thrive

we're sitting together
watching the kites
chasing the breeze
all looking for height

couples are strolling
she takes his hand
the smiling faces
all summer tanned

I can smell bacon
from a little cafe
I order a sarnie
my dog getting half

when it's the time
go to the Wheat
have a few pints
my friends to meet

It's one Sunday morning
you feel you're alive
this world can be good
a place to thrive

MY DARLING FRIEND

strange orange glow
trees are on the march
wind refuses to blow
the flowers corrupt
turn black in default

from start to finish
is this the end

why didn't they listen
those caught out in the street
they all turn to salt

is this what becomes of me

from start to finish
is this the end

have one one
my darling friend

clouds holding tears
rivers are in reverse
oceans stop to fear
the trees are naked
they pressed reset

from start to finish
is this the end

I didn't see it coming
those caught out in the street
they all turn to salt

can there be more than this

from start to finish
is this the end

have another one
my darling friend

SILVER DARLINGS

Herring shoals

we leave the harbour
on our way
sun is shining
gulls are screaming
smell the fish in the air
the boat she rolls
we catch the breeze
I smile
to first mate Johnny Dole

were on the run
our hearts they sing
we follow in search
of the silver darling

I'm trusting the sea
all the swell
the high waves
the foam the spray
we go on their trail
follow the shoals
take in the wind
I wave
to first mate Johnny Dole

it is all I remember
life at sea
it's in my heart
everything I feel
follow silver darlings
deep in my soul
without regrets
my friend
and first mate Johnny Dole

were on the run
our hearts they sing
we follow in search
of the silver darling

PEIRA CAVA

we entered the room
to atmosphere smiling
the hum of laughter and conversation
shown to a table
that looked down the valley
I was drawn to her eyes
we held hands over the table
below our feet entwine

we are high in the mountains
near Peira Cava
she is the girl
I want to spend my time with
she is the girl I love

wild mushroom soup
rose vin de maison
famous daube stew with fresh raviolis
and blueberry tart
cuisine heart of the Provance
after we strolled together
breathe the cool mountain air
with our hearts in song

soon on the journey
back to the coast
the twisting roads and hairpin bends
in the distance
Nice and the Mediterranean
it's sparking sea of azur
matching your eyes of blue
and my love for you

we were high in the mountains
near Peira Cava
she is the girl
I want to spend my time with
she is the girl I love

BALLAD OF THE MOON

There's no hope in this life
It doesn't cater for a working man
It's all set up for the titled and rich
the gentry of this land

my love taken to a prison cell
committed a crime that was so bad
a red rose he stole to bring to me
he found he was to be a dad

the sentence passed
was cruel and long
my love I won't see soon
a 10 year stretch
Australia bound

he may as well have sent you to the moon

how can they be so cruel
your unborn child will you ever see?
he sailed away to a land that's young
so far across the sea

the judge pounded on his gable
in anger passed the worst he can
'you people deserve to go to hell
for stealing the rights of man'

the sentence passed
was cruel and long
all forsake of a bloom
a 10 year stretch
Australia bound

he may as well have sent you to the moon
oh! my love my sweetest love
he may as well have sent you to the moon

The newspapers reported
this heinous crime
he should've been taken down,
flogged and strung up high
to take a flower from Lord St Clair
is evil beyond repair

the sentence passed
was cruel and long
I'm left here in my gloom
a 10 year stretch
Australia bound

he may as well have sent you to the moon
he may as well have sent you to the moon

TOURS OF DUTY

G.I. Blues

In the jungles of north Vietnam
the Cong have got our number
we've got to try and keep awake
take a pill to keep from slumber

there all around us everywhere
these Gooks get in our brains
this one country's gone to hell
to survive I mainline my veins

will you be waiting for me sweetheart
will you wait till I get home

In the dessert of Southern Iraq
looks like we've got them beat
we bombed the shit out of them
stuck in stinking God dam heat

you don't know who's a friend
or who wants to fuck with you
we're sent to be their saviour
but they hate everything we do

will you be waiting for me sweetheart
will you wait till I get home

on these beaches at Normandy
we are there to beat that Hun.
bullets flying friends are dying
get them bastards on the run

every road now goes to Berlin
Russians moves from the east
it won't be long before it's over
we'll kill forever the Nazi beast

will you be waiting for me sweetheart
will you wait till I get home

A SON'S FATHER

oh! Father I know you said
I should have done more at school
or I could end up just like you
doing a job that just sees you through

but Father you haven't done that bad
you don't owe a penny to any man
and no man owes to you

oh! Father I know you said
I should've travelled all the world
not stay at home just like you
I should see how others live their lives

but Father do you need to travel far
and see all the sights of the world
to find who you really are

Father Father you've never grown up
I believe I'm older than you

oh! Father I know you said
you will be lucky to find true love
like finding a nugget of gold
never give up the search

but Father you've found your luck
married to my mum for 45 years
that must count as gold

Father Father you've never grown up
I believe I'm older than you

oh! Father I know you said
treat every man as how you find
if he sweeps the street well
give him respect for that

but Father you see no difference
with paupers, peasants or kings
and I believe your right

Father Father you are right!
I believe we've both grown up!

A BIT OF DIRT

six o'clock the whistle blows
you climb the ladder to hell
over the wall bayonets locked
too many men they fell

thunder claps of cannon fire
bullets screeching our ears
greying faces of terrified men
running to face their fears

was it worth all the cost
for a bit of dirt
too many brave men
shot to bits
so many friends we lost

men scream where they fall
wish they could be blessed
grown men their mothers call
to be close to her breast

all this death and madness
to gain a few metres of dirt
souls left to rot on the field
loved ones left to hurt

was it worth all the cost
for a bit of dirt
too many brave men
shot to bits
so many friends we lost

CRITICAL MASS

the time has come
I knew it would
I need to get away
get out of this race
escape to the hills
walk in the heather
let the wind rip my face

my mind it races
the game is up
my stomach churns
like the angry bees
in a hostile hive
they are coming
I go weak in the knees

I carry this load
I shiver and chill
a critical mass
on a Highland hill

there's no escape
nowhere to run
I will try and hide
it's a matter of time
before I'm caught
I will have to pay
for my ghastly crime

I carry this load
I shiver and chill
a critical mass
on a Highland hill

SHIVER AND CHILL

Adapted for song

the time has come
I knew it would
got to get away
escape the hood

my mind it races
my game is up
stomach churns
I'm all fucked up

I carry this load
I shiver and chill
It broke my heart
my mind caved in

there's no escape
nowhere to run
I will try and hide
I've got my gun

danger all around
they're after me
thoughts of you
where I shud be

I carry this load
I shiver and chill
It broke my heart
my mind caved in

I did my wrong
with double cross
a contracts out
done by my boss

they're after me
I knew they might
I won't give up
without a fight

I carry this load
I shiver and chill
It broke my heart
my mind caved in

THE SWEETEST MISTRESS

It may be days
weeks or months
that you ignore her love
she will wait she is pure
you can't resist her charms

she can be the sweetest mistress
but if you tangle in her web
she can sap all your strength
lead you to your lowest ebb

she can be the sweetest mistress
but if you tangle in her web
she can sap your inner strength
and drag you down
drag you down

Spent the night
deep in her arms
wake late in the morn
consumed with guilt
won't go to her no more

she can be the sweetest mistress
but if you tangle in her web
she can sap your strength
lead you to your lowest ebb

she can be the sweetest mistress
but if you tangle in her web
she can sap your inner strength
and drag you down
drag you down

she won't take no for answer
she never gives her love for free
she'll always come back to haunt you
she can be the sweetest mistress
and drag you down
drag you down

BLACK HOLES

In Camberley

the snow rages it's minus four
my head it aches my eyes burn
vicious talk disturbs the peace
what was said must not return

this is why we get black holes
to gather all the useless words

all the trees are dark and bare
the sky's heavy filled with grey
all these wires that got crossed
useless words wrecked the day

this is why we get black holes
to gather all the useless words

all those who abuse their love
for them will be no parting kiss
a hole appears from the earth
drags them all to the dark abyss

this is why we get black holes
to gather all the useless words

THE VILLAGE GREEN

our perfect little village
with thatched roofs
and one little pub
on the village green

let them park their tents
on the cricket pitch
all God's children
on the village green

come to our pretty village
it has to be seen
in England's heartland
with our village green

build a mosque for them
come from the east
our starving friends
to the village green

eat the ducks and swans
from the village pond
build latrines for them
on the village green

take them in our houses
join the cricket team
marry our daughters
on the village green

come to our pretty village
it has to be seen
in England's heartland
with our village green

CRUEL ENVY

in shadowy darkness
who needs another hour?
swirling mist in my room
clouds my vision

there are no colours.
in my garden
then I think of what I am
and the damage I caused

with my tongue

my future ripped apart
I twisted loves dreams
with cruel envy

in depressing gloom
who needs another day?
the dark fog's all around
murk's my sanity

there are no smiles
on their faces
then I think of who I am
and the damage I caused

just being around

my future ripped apart
I twisted loves dreams
with cruel envy

INVISIBLE CAGE

I hate to see, birds stuck in a cage
all day on a perch, staring at mirrors
they have their wings
but no room to fly

I hate to see, bears stuck in a cage
round in circles, slowly going mad
forced to do tricks
to make us laugh

I hate to see, cats stuck in a cage
pace back and fore, nowhere to go
all need to run free
and be who they are

inside I'm filled, deep with rage
ashamed I do nothing
from my invisible cage

I hate what happens, to majestic whales
the sad ocean is their freedom cage
hunt them all down
until there're all gone

I hate what happens, to grand elephants
poached and chased for ivory tusks
they steal their lives
for nothing but greed

inside I'm filled, deep with rage
ashamed I do nothing
from my invisible cage

IN A WAR THAT THEY WON

here come the boys
disembark the train
in a war that they won
returning as heroes

they left with waves
their smiling faces
adventures they seek
full of young hope

no one told them
what they would find
no one told them
the horrors to see

they're not our boys
who left on the train
in a war that they won
but at so much cost?

tears stream down
blank looks on faces
their brave comrades
that they left behind

no one told them
what they would find
no one told them
the horrors to see

some bear the scars
with others no limbs
these dark memories
will never be gone

my happy young lad
who left for the fight
in a war that they won
now he is broken

no one told them
what they would find
no one told them
the horrors to see

HEY BILLY

What a day
dry as a bone
could kill for pint
will see you mate
don't be late
see ya down
The Rose and Crown

Hey Billy
get 'em in
mines a pint of Mandela (Stella)

Day is done
I got a thirst
could murder a pint
will see you mate
don't be late
your buying
at the Red lion

Hey Billy
get 'em in
mines a pint of Britney (beer)

On way home
need to hydrate
could swing for a pint
will see you mate
don't be late
see ya Jock
at the Fighting Cock

Hey Billy
get 'em in
mines a pint of Jagger (lager)

Six pints
get 'em down
I need some more
with all my mates
right states
great folk
at the Royal Oak

Hey Billy
get 'em in
I'm Brahms and Lyst (Pissed)

CHILDREN YOU GOT TO STOP

children you got to stop
children you got to stop
you got to enjoy your lives
no more killin'
on the streets of London

I want to hold my boy
I want to see my boy again
when will I see my boy again?

children stop all this killin'
children stop all the stabbin'
got to be safe to walk around
no more killin'
on the streets of London

I want to hold my boy
I want to see my boy again
when will I see my boy again?

children put your guns away
children put your knives away
you all need to have a future
no more killin'
on the streets of London

I want to hold my boy
I want to see my boy again
when will I see my boy again?

look at all your mother's tears
look at all your mother's grief
all her future`s gone with you
no more killin'
on the streets of London
no more killin'

on the streets of Kingston
no more killin'
on the streets of Mexico
no more killin'
on the streets of Manila
no more killin'
on the streets of Caracas

I want to hold my boy
I want to see my boy again
when will I see my boy again?

SLEEPING ROUGH

spare a little thought
If you see him sleeping rough
you don't know his story
he may have lost his love?
or lost his former glory?

spare a little thought
If you see him sit on a bench
his eyes blank and lost
no home fire waits for him
just the cold and frost

don't let me hear you say
that he's a down and out
he's lost a little bit of luck
things not turned his way

don't sneer at him
with his can of special brew
it may be the only thing
to get him through his day
a little comfort bring

you can smile at him
it's not going to hurt anyone
he needs a turn of luck
so can you lend your hand?
to get his life unstuck

don't let me hear you say
that he's a down and out
he's lost a little bit of luck
things not turned his way

WAR ZONES

where go all our soldier boys
they're on the way to fight a war
they march with rifles
to shoot and kill
some won't come home
these soldier boys
left in graves
in a foreign land

where go all our sailor boys
they're on the way to fight a war
their ships have guns
to shoot and kill
some won't come home
these sailor boys
been taken by
the hungry sea

where go all our flying boys
they're on the way to fight a war
fly their Spitfires
to shoot and kill
some won't come home
these flying boys
all blown up
in the open sky

where go now our bonnie lads
out in these naked jungle streets
their guns and knives
to shoot and kill
some won't come home
these bonnie lads
taken down
in London streets

THE TEARS I HIDE

look at the clown
he's playing the fool
they're all laughing
the painted rouge
pretends to smile

they don't see behind his eyes
they don't see the tears he hides

look at that girl
dressed to the nines
makeup is perfect
the white powder
hiding the lines

they don't see behind her eyes
they don't see the tears she hides

look at the Jester
jokes for the crowd
knowing the tricks
to win your heart
and take you in

they don't see behind his eyes
they don't see the tears he hides

just look at me
come with a smile
outside I'm laughing
but torn up inside
I'm torn inside

you don't see behind my eyes
you don't see the tears I hide

they don't see behind their eyes
they don't see the tears they hide

LOTUS FLOWER

Jung Yi a loves fiery temptress
let me be under your control
the Virgin Mary lost her ticket (knickers)
her barren womb will be sold

Sister Benedict's silver crucifix
oh for sanctuary in your arms
corpse reviver sad Mary Shelly
her collection of death charms

I love you more
by the hour
In your hair a lotus flower

Aphrodite came here to gorge
her chalice screams for more
Ophelia has drank too much
lying naked behind her door

Valkyrie all her beautiful ruins
in retreat this Dresden flower
Taurus with bull shot anger
steals the secret to her power

I love you more
by the hour
In your hair a lotus flower

Bacchus your sweet wine flows
we indulge with drunken orgy
Claudius with street abandon
he stayed behind an absentee

Indra with all her storm clouds
Warmongers smile their wrath
the Buddha lies down to prey
searching for enlightened path

I love you more
by the hour
In your hair a lotus flower

WHO WE ARE

All our boys of the terrier breed
we will not let them beat us sister
together we will sing songs of war
songs of love and victory
oh! Rosie, I'm sorry what I did to you
can I call you when this is over

and we'll remember who we are!

All our lads who heed the call
defeat is not an option brother
all our hearts will beat as one
our lives linked together
oh! Rosie, all I think about is you
can I call you when this is over

and we'll remember who we are!

Tomorrow we go over the wall at six
these trenches a hell hole mother
so much pain and smell of death
nobody can ever win here
oh! Rosie, all I think about is you
can I call you if I make it over

and we'll remember who we are!

I lay in this ditch with my thoughts
remembering what you said father
'there is no glory to be found in war
many souls will be taken'
oh! Rosie, I'm still in love with you
can I call you if I make it over

and we'll remember who we are!

Men they gathered from all around
they fought to save our nation
their Standard was a raging lion
the colour they choose was blue
oh! Rosie, lets raise a glass together
and toast our Heroes past and new

and we'll remember who we are!

PANTA SANTA

Daddy! Daddy!
why's the doggy called Big Red?
Panta Santa! Panta Santa!
Daddy! Daddy!
why's the doggy called Big Red?
Panta Santa! Panta Santa!
it's 'cause I found the doggy
smiling in a bush!

Panta Santa! Panta Santa!
come have some Christmas tapas with me!

Daddy! Daddy!
why's the doggie got a makeup bag
Panta Santa! Panta Santa!
Daddy! Daddy!
why's the doggie got a makeup bag
Panta Santa! Panta Santa!
it's 'cause the little doggie
has got his lipstick out

Panta Sant! Panta Santa!
come have some Christmas tapas with me!

Daddy! Daddy!
why's the doggie got three legs
Panta Santa! Panta Santa!
Daddy! Daddy!
why's the doggie got three legs
Panta Santa! Panta Santa!
It's 'cause the little doggie
is sitting on a stool

Panta Sant! Panta Santa!
come have some Christmas tapas with me!

Daddy! Daddy!
why's the doggie thinks he's Star Wars
Panta Santa! Panta Santa!
Daddy! Daddy!
why's the doggie think he's Star Wars
Panta Santa! Panta Santa!
It's 'cause the little doggie
is Toby One Kenobi

Panta Sant! Panta Santa!
come have some Christmas tapas with me!

A DARK SHADE OF BLUE

I woke this morning
our bed a solitary place to be
darkness in my soul
sadness clouds the sunrise
I feel very down today

The sun is going down
clouds gather round
and the sky is turning
a very very dark shade of blue

I woke this morning
our bed a desolate place to be
sorrow is all around
bleakness clouds the dawning
I feel very down today

I woke this morning
alone where you used to be
despair creeps over me
I miss you so desperately
I feel very lonely today

The sun is going down
clouds gather round
and the sky is turning
a very very dark shade of blue

KING RAT LA LOTTE

We don't have da freedom
for all that we fought
there no place safe now
everywhere we caught
we scared of dat man
he send his Obea men
to come for da money
something we no got
we all scared of da man
King Rat la Lotte

King Rat La Lotte
he come take everything
King Rat La Lotte
he takes all we got
King Rat la Lotte
he come for da children
an leave em out to rot

We have ta rise up again
dis trouble gotta stop
they gotta learn respect
like old mama taught
we find a vodoo spell
inflict them Obea men
no scared of dat man
nothing that hes got
he gonna catch a bullet

King Rat La Lotte
King Rat La Lotte
he come take everything
King Rat La Lotte
he takes all we got
King Rat la Lotte
he come for da children
an leave em out to rot

ANCIENT LOVE

At the top of the Hill of Fairies
we were haunted by the view
Brahan Seer keeps it under lock and key
no Spirit can ever escape there
when 7 bridges cross the River Ness
fire will run through the streets
and blood will surely follow

We held each other's trembling hands
our bodies close in warm embrace
we gazed into each other's smiling eyes
and we knew why we stood here
we had discovered Love

Standing next to our beautiful Flora
gazing down the path of the Ness
she helped escape her Bonnie Charlie
disguised him as a spinning maid
they landed safe on Portree Haven
away from the Evil Cumberland

Standing on desolate Culloden Moor
Jacobite dreams were slaughtered
followed blind the Young Pretender
the British Throne his birthright
we felt the presence of many a ghost
who never found their peace there

On the Banks of the Caledonian Canal
following the steps of Thomas Telfor
he joined the coasts from east to west
provided work for starving thousands
watched in awe at the sailing ships
bringing gold and silk and silver

We held each other's trembling hands
our bodies close in warm embrace
we gazed into each other's smiling eyes
and we knew why we stood here
we had discovered Love

HOUDINI'S PUNCH

Red telephone boxes
smelt of piss
I never saw it coming
Houdini's Punch

she not going to join me
she's flying south
following her dreams
dreams I don't belong

my mind was numb
a marching zombie
owned by the night
the hail, the sleet
the maggot wind
the dreich

Houdini's punch
garroting my guts
twisting, strangling
tighter and tighter
the bile rising
I needed to vomit
I wanted to scream!
howl!
but nothing came out

I arrived
at I don't know where
or how I got there
I didn't care
I had lost the night
I had lost my love

she not going to join me
she's flying south
following her dreams
dreams I don't belong

YOUR MOTHER'S ARMS

She was first to hold you close
the first to see you smile
when you fell she'd pick you up
comfort you with mother's style
there for all the growing years
of building towers and dinosaurs
the wonder of these Lego bricks
the magic of your first Star Wars

In your life
you will have broken bones
or even have a broken heart
you might live by the crucifix
or rely on lucky charms
but you will never feel
a love so pure
as in your Mother's arms

There for all the schooling days
glowing pride at graduation
your fist job, first lovers tiff
her shoulder there to lean on
waving desperate tears goodbye
when you were called to arms
every night sleep won't come
until your home and free from harm

One day you will present to her
a little baby so bright and new
all the love will shine from her
that same love she gave to you
kindly listen what I have to say
but don't dwell there for long
cherish the time you have with her
because one day she will be gone
one day your Mother she will be gone

In your life
you will have broken bones
or even have a broken heart
you might find religion
or rely on lucky charms
but you will never feel
a love so pure
as in your Mother's arms

NO CHRISTMAS TIME IN DIXIE

It's Christmas time in Dixie
we can all meet and play
Pa and me join the turkey shoot
for the feast on Christmas day
sister Jenny, Paul and Clem
and all the kids are here
Pa pours out his Christmas rye
Ma she cooks our favourite treat
lemon custard and cranberry pie

Come join us here for Christmas
a time to rejoice
a warm welcome in the Southern States
awaits you here in Dixie

My name is Vestal Stanton
I was born in Tennessee
I've been called up to fight a war
to protect these States of Dixie
Pa told me to have respect
be honest with yourself
It is in the South I want to be
and I know that I have to fight
believing we should all be free

We had our first encounter
the battle of Wilson's Creek
beat them good these Union boys
there was no joy for me to speak
I lost my best pal Joseph
was the bravest honest lad
he caught a bullet to the head
grieve for his loving Marianne
his four kids their daddy dead

Don't come here for Christmas
no time to rejoice
no welcome here in the Southern States
only bullets here in Dixie

I've witnessed so much pain
for my young tender years
was on the hill when Atlanta fell
Pickett's charge at Gettysburg
fought them hand to hand
I saw the fear in their eyes
but one thing I learned for free
is when they screamed in pain
they sound just like you and me

All of these great Generals
Jackson, Anderson and Lee
they were proud and solid South
made promises we couldn't see
said it would soon be over
but all I see is heroes blood
mixed up with pure white snow
they lied to us to make us fight
didn't tell what we should know

Don't come here for Christmas
no time to rejoice
no welcome here in the Southern States
only bullets here in Dixie

Oh! this bloody war at last
it has been lost and won
we paid a price for this freedom
what a terrible toll was done
one million souls were lost
what is it that you believe?
well it seems pretty clear to me
this should never happen again
and all wars should cease to be

I only wish this could be true
if all the slaves now free
could come and join us here for Christmas
and pray together for all who was lost
in theses great States of Dixie

LORD PROTECT OUR LOVE

You smile at me
the flame in your pale green eyes
lights up your tanned fragile face
you reach out your hand to touch me
you are wearing perfect silk and lace
I awake to the chorus of singing birds
as the Sun breaks through the misty dawn
I turn and tell you I love you
until there is no sparkle left in the eyes of the night sky
or the sun melts the heart of the cold cold moon

Oh! Lord Protect Our Love!

You put your arms around me
you tell me that you love me
you untie your perfect silk and lace
we cling to each other like limpets
terrorized by the seas merciless face
the wind turns her head and smiles
and provides a cool gentle breeze
time himself lends his helping hand
and slows down his rigid pace
I will caress the locks of your golden hair
I will kiss the sweetness in your eyes
I will taste our burning passion
I will cling to our embrace
and standing there above us
is Aphrodite the Goddess of Love
holding hands with a Templar Knight
sent by the Lord above
they are here to help and guide us
they are here to protect our Love

Oh! Lord Protect our Love!

THE PRISON

She held my arm tightly
with both her hands
her face was pale
with a hint of pink on her cheeks
a single tear trickled down
she was usually so strong
always in control
I gently pulled away
she released her grip
I turned around
there was no pleasure
in my control
no pleasure at all
I did not look behind
I kept on walking
there was no magnetic pull
dragging me back
nothing
I was free
free from the prison
that was her

I'LL BE HERE FOR YOU

when you can't get out of bed
staying in your room instead
you see dark clouds
when the sky is blue

I'll be here for you

when you can't go out to walk
take my arm I'll be your rock
I will never give up
what I have to do

I'll be here for you

when you feel you don't belong
you have done nothing wrong
you can count on me
to make you strong

I'll be here for you

whenever you are feeling down
I'll be here to be that clown
and make you laugh
to stop your frown

I'll be here for you

S.O.S.

With her black leather gear
and her silver cross
on her back
a tattoo of Kurt Cobain
all she wants
is to run with the pack
be part of the gang
so she gets herself down
and takes matters in hand
she'll take it like a man
but one thing's for sure
she's no Pussy Galore

and she won't spit
she'll swallow

With her green spiked hair
and her bullet belt
on her back
a tattoo of Joey Ramone
all she wants
is to run with the pack
be part of the gang
so she gets herself down
her way of getting ahead
she'll take it like a man
one thing about her
she no Honeysuckle Rider

and she won't spit
she'll swallow

With her winged deaths head
and her Angels code
on her back
a tattoo of the Grateful Dead

all that she wants
is to run with the pack
be part of the gang
so she gets herself down
a mama has to be fed
she'll take it like a man
but one thing that's freaky
she's no Kissy Suzuki

and she won't spit
she'll swallow

alternate end

when today is tomorrow
and it's time to come
she'll fly away with the swallow

ALL THE KING'S HORSES

There she goes
spinning up to the clouds
holding colours
sharing with Lucy's sparkling sky
gyrating so fast
on her Carnival ride
out of control

all the King's horses
can't bring her back

There she goes
almost touching the stars
blitzing memories
fuelled by the Archers amber shot
tangling in webs
trying to get home
out of control

all the King's horses
can't bring her back

There she goes
grabbing on to the moon
scared to let go
using the strength of Stella's grip
dazzled and giddy
on roller coaster trip
out of control
all the King's horses
can't bring her back

There she goes
tumbling down to earth
holding flowers
burning up the ice in her veins

tired and sleepy
she dances a waltz
out of control

all the King's horses
can't bring her back

There she goes,
dancing like ember fires
soothing and moving
forbidden to taste,
free from love
like a raging storm
out of control

There she goes
she's lost in the forest
her lonely bed
a carpet of jasmine and lilies
Special Forces
there to protect her
finding her path

all the King's horses
can't bring her back

She lost her heart to the Knave of Spades
all the Kings horses can't bring her back

all the King's horses
all the King's Men
can't bring her back

THE TOWER

I had to take the chance
go and search myself
leave behind all that cushy life
say goodbye to all my friends
and all my family
there always comes a time
you have to prove yourself
or I will never be fulfilled
with never a regret
it's easier to stay at home
in the comfort of the ones I love

and I've never felt so all alone
I want to hold my baby
I turn around
and in the distance
I always see the Tower

They work you hard
I'm not shy of work
I will show them what I can do
when the work is all done
I will hit the Bar
search deep into my wine
stop my mind playing tricks
stop these thoughts of home
soon get their visa
and husband and my baby
again be in these arms of mine

and I've never felt so all alone
I want to hold my baby
I turn around
and in the distance
I always see the Tower

Then into Purple Heather

'I will build, my love a tower
by the cool crests of waters
and I'll cling to her forever
like the ivy to the heather
will you go, lassie, go

and we'll all go together
to pick, wild mountain thyme
all along the purple heather
will you go, lassie go
lassie, go

will you go, lassie, go'

Conclusion

The best news it came
is it just a dream
can I start to live again
be with the ones I love
hold my baby close
the time it has come
I have passed the test
the greatest test of all
with never a regret
I look to the future
in the comfort of the ones I love

and I've never felt so good before
soon to hold my baby
I turn around
and in the distance
I see the Tower smile

NEVER MEANT TO BE

A warrior Nation
bound by the traditions
of Samurai cult
never to surrender
they'd rather fall on the soul
of their sacred swords
it took the horrors of Nagasaki
the rage of a 'divine wind'
4,000 dead brave young pilots
honoured to release a Nation
from all the shackles
of its glorious past

an illusion never meant to be

Born of traditions
of many centuries gone
in western worlds
there's nothing to compare
she's no hooker or courtesan
bows with subtle grace
perfect face of alabaster white
lips a heart of ruby red
kimono dress of the purist silks
you she's bound to serve
our beautiful Geisha
never there to marry

an illusion never meant to be

Can this be sport
or is it a martial art
two giant gods
of hulking sex appeal
stamp feet like water buffalos
raging in their heat

all that modesty is covered
by diphers coloured black
they will offer salt to the wind
for to cleanse the past
the art of the Sumo
Olympics never be

an illusion never meant to be

You could have landed
on a another planet
landed on the moon
things are done a little different
in the land of the rising sun

PLATO O PLOMO

Silver or Lead

Born near the city of Medellin
from poverty he rose to fame
the richest man in Columbia
that is what they claim
his money came from selling drugs
tons of the stuff he sold
cocaine the designer drug of choice
nose candy so I'm told
if you stood in his way
it was either silver or lead
a pocket full of dollars
or a bullet in the head

No escape from Escobar
no place you can go
he has all the money
got from selling blow
he owns the cops and judges
all the people too
there's no escape from Pablo's men
only death for you

At the height of all his powers
60 million he took each day
what to do with this money
how do you hide it away
houses he built for the very poor
football fields for play
he built a hacienda called Napoles
for all his gang to stay
imported wild animals
opulence was plain to see
money never an object
but was he really free

His aim to be a politician
to help the poor and underfed
the man who exposed his truth
they killed that man dead
Galan the future for the country
extradite cartel thugs
he was murdered by Pablo's men
all to protect their drugs
next candidate in line
was due to fly in a plane
a bomb was put onboard
the country went insane

a crazy deal to stop the terror
he received a sentence short
he even built his 5 star prison
never even went to court
they found away to get to him
that plan he was told
and he escaped out into the night
Escobar they could not hold
DEA, the other Cartels
they all wanted him dead
no Plata choice for him
just 3 bullets in the head

LOVE NEVER COMPETES

To 007

As soon as you saw him
you knew he was the one
dark sophistication
an aura
that stands out from the crowd
a life full of mystery
secrets, intrigue
he takes you to places
you only dreamed
fly down to Rio
Coco Cabana beach
ski in the mountains
at St Moritz
he has already taken
most of your heart
you have given everything
a woman can give

Oh! please beware
Silvy Killdare
is there a soul behind his dark eyes
you are already under his will
all that you give
love never competes
with a license to kill

You are drawn to him
like moth to a flame
dark sophistication
his wit
strikes like a rapier blade
cocktails are drunk
shaken not stirred
he takes you to places
you only dreamed

midnight train from Moscow
Orient Express
cards at the Casino
Monte Carlo or bust
he has already taken
the life that you had
used for his pleasure
his every whim

Oh! please beware
Silvy Killdare
is there a soul behind his dark eyes
you are here in your free will
all that you give
love never competes
with a license to kill

DANCE WITH ME

Mamy!
why do they always have to fight?
is this the way it has to be?
why can't they just come over here?
and dance with me!

little boys in party mood
playing their games of tag and chase
each is given a big balloon
all around the room they race
screaming shouts the game has turned
the balloon becomes a weapon
to hit each other in the face

big boys always want to win
in their hands are sticks and stones
the game played far too rough
bruised arms and broken bones
the game has turned now out of hand
kid is hit and down he falls
lying there he cries and moans

teen boys join in the gang
initiation rites are to hurt someone
in their pockets carry knifes
purpose not to have some fun
they want to fight the other gangs
join together to hurt and stab
beat them down and see them run

join the army to be a man
play with guns there're made to kill
training time it will be hard
soon to use your lethal skill
you are free to go and kill someone
use your bullets or hand to hand
time to enjoy and get your thrill

Mamy!
why do they always have to fight?
is this the way it has to be?
why can't they just come over here?
and dance with me!

BPC

The Clans gathered round
travelled many a mile
there to meet a Bonnie Prince
home from foreign exile
back to lead his cheering men
return to us our Scottish pride
will never again relinquish
win back his rightful crown
stolen by the English

we will follow blind
this merry band
follow our Bonnie Charlie
into the heart of England

The battle at Prestonpans
victory for us to start
the glorious march down south
thru middle England's heart
we were a riotous merry band
all in sight of London's reach
the height of all our powers
one great final push for us
and the prize is ours

we will follow blind
this merry band
follow our Bonnie Charlie
into the heart of England

We waited far too long
for our friend ally France
no help from them ever came
had we lost our chance
many men they just got bored
and we were forced to retreat

it was soon very clear to see
that great Jacobite dream
was never meant to be

A last desperate stand
desolate Culloden Moor
all the men were tired and beat
finished that's for sure
our Prince's dreams in tatters
we are left for cannon fodder
one final brave last stand
not one prisoner was taken
by butcher Cumberland

oh! where are you now
Young Pretender
back safe in exile's haven
leaving us here to suffer

Soon the soldiers came
all these bloody English
in their uniforms of scarlet red
they had a job to finish
why did they steal all our food?
and burn down our little crofts
leaving us with all this pain
families turned out to face
a howling winter's rain

oh! where are you now
Young Pretender
back safe in exile's haven
leaving us here to suffer

IT DOESN'T MATTER IF IT RAINS

When you ever get bad thoughts
I will tell them go and shoo!
I don't have time for lots friends
I don't even need a few
I'm only happy with my one girl
I don't want anybody new

I don't care if the sun don't shine
it doesn't matter if it rains
as long as I'm with you

I don't like when you are scared
I wouldn't even tell you boo!
when I'm alone and by myself
a ship without its crew
I'm here to give you all my love
it's something that your due

I don't care if the sun don't shine
it doesn't matter if it rains
as long as I'm with you

When you're standing next to me
my heart can't help but coo!
when I see that smile of yours
there is no better view
if you ask me what it's all about
I reply that you're the clue

I will do without another whiskey
don't need any other brew
I will never tell you any lies
nothing that's untrue
and when I see that you are sad
I will tell a joke or two

I don't care if the sun don't shine
it doesn't matter if it rains
as long as I'm with you

I will be with you until end of time
together we're stuck like glue!
I live my life with you together
I will see it through
If you ask that same old question
I reply 'I love you too!'

I don't care if the sun don't shine
it doesn't matter if it rains
as long as I'm with you

FIRE IN HIS EYES

To Andy Murray

You can see the fire
the fire in his eyes
you can see the fire in his eyes
nothing is going to stop him now
he's going all the way

this time he's going to make it
this time he'll see it through

you can see the fire in his eyes

He's tasted bitter loss before
never has he crossed that line
he'll do it for the folks back home
they've suffered far too long for this

you can see the fire in his eyes
soon he will touch the sun
higher than he's ever been
he waited all his life for this
it's taken all his hopes and dreams
you can see the fire in his eyes

This time he will make it
this time he will make it through
you can see the fire
the fire in his eyes
you can see the fire in his eyes

this time he's going to make it
this time he'll see it through
he's given everything he's got
everything and more

Andy Murray is number 1
he gave us all his heart

ABOUT THE AUTHOR

I was born in Inverness in 1949 and have lived there until 1969. I moved to East Kilbride for a year and then to London, (near Heathrow). I lived in London until I retired in 2009, except for a ten year period in the eighties and early nineties, when I lived in Saudi Arabia. I have worked most of my life in the Airline Industry which enabled me to travel the world quite easily and cheaply. I am now retired and have lived in Spain for the last ten years.

I only started writing since I retired in 2009 and in the last few years have assembled over four hundred poems / songs. I have selected what I believe are the best. It has been an amazing ride for someone who, until a few years ago had never put pen to paper. Hardly a day went by that I did not come up with a new poem or song. Mostly I woke during the night and before I knew it I had a couple of verses written on my phone. I would transfer on to my PC and finish what I started as soon as I got up.

I really enjoy it and there is still no let up on my output. It keeps my old brain cells going.

My influences are really all the Rock poets, especially Bob Dylan, Leonard Cohen, Ian Curtis etc. and maybe a little Rabbie Burns.

MORE FROM

WORDCATCHERpublishing

We publish a variety of titles in many genres.
Please visit our website for details of current
submission guidelines:

www.wordcatcher.com

NON FICTION
British History
Business
Personal Development
Professional Development
Politics and Current Affairs
True Stories and Real Life

FICTION
Historical Fiction
Supernatural
Crime and Thrillers
Literary Fiction

POETRY

CHILDREN'S

...and more...!

If you enjoyed this book, please take a moment to leave a review where you purchased this title and on wordcatcher.com. Reviews help other readers pick books they will enjoy, and your recommendation helps.

If you'd like to know more about the author, you can find their profile on www.wordcatcher.com

We're only human! We make mistakes.
If you notice any typos or errors, please contact us at admin@wordcatcher.com

Thank you for reading.